Sustaining the Transformation

U.S. Marine Corps

PCN 144 000075 00

DISTRIBUTION STATEMENT A: Approved for public release; distribution is unlimited.

DEPARTMENT OF THE NAVY
Headquarters United States Marine Corps
Washington, D.C. 20380-1775

28 June 1999

FOREWORD

Our Corps does two things for America: we make Marines and we win our nation's battles. Our ability to successfully accomplish the latter, of course, depends upon how well we do the former. We make Marines through a process called transformation. During this process, we change young men's and women's lives forever by imbuing them with our nation's highest ideals. Since the birth of our Corps, Marines have been forged in the crucible of our entry-level training, whether it be recruit training or Officer Candidates School. Through the years we have refined and strengthened this process in pursuit of increasingly higher standards. Those who earn the title "Marine" have been polished and honed by attentive mentoring and the application of our time-proven leadership traits and principles. Transformation does not end at the conclusion of entry-level training; it continues throughout a Marine's service—whether that service ends after a single enlistment or lasts 30 years. Marines maintain standards that are consistent with our core values of honor, courage, and commitment, and they are held accountable for maintaining the legacy of valor established by the sacrifices of those Marines who preceded them. As Marines leave our active ranks, they carry our timeless values with them back to their civilian communities, and our nation is stronger for it. This transformation, as timeless as the Corps itself, is our legacy to America.

Our Corps' survival depends upon the transformation. Young Marines enter our Corps today with as much spirit and enthusiasm as ever in our proud history. They carry within their hearts the burning embers of zeal and devotion that were lit during their first meeting with a Marine (active, reserve, retired, or former) or during their first interview with a Marine recruiter or officer selection officer. This spirit builds during recruit training or at the Officer Candidates School, and it continues to grow during Marine combat training, infantry skills training, The Basic School, and military occupational specialty training. Cohesion is carefully fostered during each of these entry-level training experiences.

Sometimes, this burning flame of enthusiasm reaches its crescendo immediately following the entry-level training pipeline, only to dim during a Marine's service with his or her first unit. Sustaining the transformation process ensures that the flame of enthusiasm does not wane, and it allows the Corps to capitalize on our most precious asset—the individual Marine.

Our warfighting capability depends upon a lasting transformation. Every Marine must possess the intellect, skill, and solid moral foundation to fight in the increasingly chaotic battlespace of the 21st century. The operational environment of tomorrow—characterized by rapidly changing threats across the spectrum of conflict, often in the course of a single day and within the space of three contiguous city blocks—will require our Marines to make correct decisions while under extreme duress and without their leaders present. The "three-block war" will challenge the decisiveness of our small-unit leaders, our "strategic corporals," in ways we may not yet fully appreciate. These small-unit leaders will play an essential role in ensuring the Corps succeeds in this chaotic environment. A successful and sustained transformation will ensure they are up to the task.

In order for the transformation to be successful, every Marine must take ownership of the process—it is every Marine's responsibility. It is an ongoing, dynamic process that begins with a Marine's first contact with a recruiter and continues throughout a Marine's life. Every Marine must understand: what the transformation is, the benefits that can be derived from it (for the individual Marine, for the unit, for the Corps, and, ultimately, for our nation), his or her place in it, and the multitude of ways he or she can effect the transformation.

Marine Corps Reference Publication (MCRP) 6-11D, *Sustaining the Transformation*, is designed to aid Marine leaders at all levels in their efforts to sustain the transformation process. It describes the phases of the transformation so that we can better understand the process, alerts us to obstacles that can impede the process, guides us in overcoming those obstacles, and provides us with examples of success. By using this publication, Marine leaders ensure that the efforts of our recruiters, drill instructors, troop handlers, and squad and section leaders are sustained, and that we provide a command climate in which all Marines can succeed.

I challenge every leader in the Corps to make both a personal and a unit commitment to sustaining the transformation. Success in our ultimate mission—victory on the battlefield—depends upon our commitment. Our Corps and our nation deserve nothing less.

C. C. KRULAK
General, U.S. Marine Corps
Commandant of the Marine Corps

DISTRIBUTION: 144 000075 00

Table of Contents

Chapter 1.   The Difference

Training Day 10	3
Training Day 15	4
Training Day 19	5
Training Day 27	7
Graduation	8
3 Months Later	11

Chapter 2.   Understanding the Transformation

Why the Transformation	18
Transformation: Phase I	20
Transformation: Phase II	21
Transformation: Phase III	23
Transformation: Phase IV	25
Transformation: Phase V	26

Chapter 3.   Cohesion

Dimensions of Cohesion	31
Individual Morale	32
Confidence in the Unit's Combat Capability	32
Confidence in Unit Leaders	33
Horizontal Cohesion	34
Vertical Cohesion	35
Mutual Support of Horizontal and Vertical Cohesion	36

Chapter 4. Obstacles and Obstacle Reduction

Section I. Obstacles
Critical Factors Affecting Sustainment   41
Quadrant Model   43
Reality-Based Unit Obstacles   44
Perception-Based Unit Obstacles   46
Reality-Based Systemic Obstacles   47
Perception-Based Systemic Obstacles   48

Section II. Obstacle Reduction
Accepting Constraints and Reality   50
Maintaining a Leadership Role   50
Understanding Leadership Principles   52
Interacting with Schools   53
Attending Unit-Level Corporal Courses   53
Encouraging Professional Military Education 54
Briefing New Joins   54
Maintaining Bachelor Enlisted Quarters   55
Providing Mentors   55
Educating Leaders   55
Drawing on External Resources   56
Utilizing the World Wide Web   56

Chapter 5. Universal Methods for Sustaining the Transformation

Command Involvement   59
Graduation and/or Unit Reception   61
In-Briefs   63
One-Month Recognition   63
Battle Anniversary   63
Unit Events   64

Unit Training and Exercises	65
Six-Month Recognition	65
Family Day	66
Deployment	66

Chapter 6.   Endstate

Definitions   73

Notes   79

Chapter 1

The Difference

"We few, we happy few, we band of brothers..."[1]

—Shakespeare

"The young American responds quickly and readily to the exhibition of qualities of leadership on the part of his officers. Some of these qualities are industry, energy, initiative, determination, enthusiasm, firmness, kindness, justness, self-control, unselfishness, honor, and courage."[2]

—General John A. Lejeune

Private James Smith only saw his brother Private Tommy Smith twice while they were first in the Marine Corps—once in the chow hall during grass week at boot camp, and then again following graduation. However, both Marines did well during recruit training and were proud of themselves and of each other. This pride was evident in their eyes and in the eyes of their parents, Mr. and Mrs. Smith, at graduation. The Smiths' felt both their boys looked and acted much older. After a short period of leave and some much-deserved rest, the Smith boys returned for training at the School of Infantry (SOI). During this training, they were in separate platoons. They saw one another occasionally, but only late in the day or on weekends.

Training Day 10

At a platoon meeting at the beginning of offense week, the squad leaders informed the privates of their future duty stations. James was going to 1st Battalion, X Marines. Since most of the platoon was going to the same battalion, the squad leader told them a little bit about their unit and where it was located. Private James Smith found out that 1/X was located at Camp X-Ray. He also was told that Marines from his new unit would link up with them later in the week. These Marines would observe training and do some initial counseling. That afternoon, the Smith boys crossed paths during offense "round robin" training. Tommy was told he would go to 2/X, which was located on the other coast. Both were disappointed that they were headed for opposite ends of the country, but they had known they would be separated sooner or later. They shook hands, wished each other luck on the 10K hike that night, then headed back to their squads.

Training Day 15

On the first day of military operations on urbanized terrain (MOUT) training, James was watching closely as his squad leader, Sergeant Brown, demonstrated window-entering techniques to the squad. When the squad broke into teams to practice the techniques demonstrated, James noticed several other Marines watching the platoon training. From a distance, they appeared to be a lieutenant, a staff sergeant, and several noncommissioned officers (NCOs). They were talking to the squad leaders and appeared to be asking a lot of questions.

Later that night, during the security patrols, Private James Smith noticed one of these Marines, a corporal, travelling with his squad. He took notice of the NCO, but did not have time to pay much attention. Private Smith had been picked to be the patrol leader, and his focus was to move the patrol along its designated route. The patrol did well in the linear danger area they encountered. The other squad members obviously had listened to their squad instruction that week because they executed their short and long security patrols without errors. It was dark by the time the patrol was safely inside friendly lines and their squad leader critiqued Private Smith and his patrol.

Immediately following the brief, the squad broke up to refill canteens and eat chow. A figure approached Private James Smith in the dark. "Private Smith," the Marine said as he extended his hand. "My name is Corporal Wilson. I will be your squad leader in A Co, 1/X. Good job on your patrol tonight. Sergeant Brown has told me a lot of good things about you. You are going to make a good addition to the squad. Go grab some chow and water. We will have some time to talk later this week. Maybe I can answer any questions you have about the unit. Again, good job, and I will see you tomorrow." Private Smith replied, "Good evening, corporal," but nothing more. He was happy about what had just taken place. The next day, James ran into his brother on his way to the MOUT fundamentals class. He told him what had happened the night before. He asked if his brother had seen or met his squad leader. Tommy looked disappointed and answered, "No, not yet."

Training Day 19

After MOUT live-fire rehearsals, James was called off to the side by Sergeant Brown. The sergeant told him to report to Corporal Wilson, who was sitting a hundred meters away on a meal, ready to eat (MRE) box looking through some folders. James hurried over and reported to the corporal. Corporal Wilson and Private James Smith spoke for some time. They discussed James' family, his training, his performance at SOI, and his physical fitness. Corporal Wilson seemed interested that James had a brother in the same class. Corporal Wilson leafed through the pages of the training folder that James had seen Sergeant Wilson use to track his test scores and training data.

After he closed the folder, Corporal Wilson began to tell James about 1/X. He told the young private that he was lucky to join a battalion with such a rich legacy. He told Private Smith of the battalion's accomplishments during World War I, of the numerous amphibious landings they had made in World War II, and how they held the line in Korea. In Vietnam, the battalion distinguished itself again in several battles and produced numerous Medal of Honor winners, three of which had been awarded to Marines in the same company that James would soon join. Corporal Wilson then explained, in detail, how the company was organized and gave an overview of the company's senior leadership. James was then told about the upcoming months of squad and platoon training, followed by two company field operations before the holidays. Corporal Wilson told James that he should be able to get home for the holidays, but that he would have to keep an eye on the duty roster. Following the holidays, the battalion would conduct a combined-arms exercise in February and deploy that following summer to Okinawa, Japan. Private James Smith was extremely happy to hear about the overseas tour because one of the reasons he joined the Corps was to travel to foreign countries.

Once Corporal Wilson was finished, James had more information than he could remember. Corporal Wilson saw the overwhelmed look in his eyes and said, "Don't worry, there isn't a test on this tomorrow. I'll see you again at graduation

Sustaining the Transformation — 7

and help you get settled into the company area. By the way, if your folks are coming to graduation, they are more than welcome to come over to the battalion area afterwards. We'll be passing out maps after the ceremony. They can head over to the battalion chow hall for noon chow where they can meet with the battalion commander and the sergeant major. Any questions for me?"

James could not think of any questions that the corporal hadn't already answered. He shook his head and said, "No, corporal." Corporal Wilson said, "All right then, pay attention at your live-fire ambush patrols next week. One more thing, the battalion is sending over a truck the morning of graduation to help with your trash. So don't throw any of your gear away just because it won't fit in your sea bag. Put it on the truck and we'll get it over to the company barracks."

James went back to training feeling good and looking forward to the future. Although the training had been tough and almost 4 months long, he could see a light at the end of the tunnel and couldn't wait to join his new unit.

Training Day 27

At the water bull, halfway through the 20K hike, the Smith brothers met again. Private Tommy Smith still had little information on his new unit. The only thing he knew was that a gunnery sergeant from his unit would be out to talk to them.

On Friday, the gunnery sergeant spoke to Tommy and about 25 other Marines en masse who were headed to 2/X. He went over the unit's history and schedule. When he was done, Tommy was dismissed, and the gunny then spoke to seven of the Marines who were headed to Company F. Tommy was slated for Company G.

Graduation

The day that both brothers had been looking forward to for so long had finally arrived—graduation day. Their parents had travelled a long way to see their sons' graduation and to wish them well as they moved on to yet another adventure.

The graduation ceremony was full of music and Marine Corps customs. Officers and staff NCOs were dressed in their Service C uniforms. James noticed the same officer and staff NCOs he had seen in the field, Corporal Wilson, and several other NCOs were sitting up front. When the guest of honor was introduced, James swore he had heard the lieutenant colonel's name before. He then heard the announcer say that the lieutenant colonel was the commanding officer of 1/X, his unit. James thought the lieutenant colonel had a hard, tough facial expression and graying hair that caused him to look older than his dad. But the lieutenant colonel looked like he was in good shape. His commanding officer praised the Marines for the hard work that had brought them this far, and he congratulated them on their accomplishments. He welcomed those new Marines who were coming to his battalion, and he went over some of the battles and victories Corporal Wilson had discussed with James during their meeting. After the speech, the commanding officer invited the families to lunch in the battalion area and told them the graduates would join their families in the afternoon.

Upon conclusion of the ceremony, the Smith brothers were exhilarated and quickly made their way over to their folks. After some time was spent slapping backs and posing for photos, the boys knew they needed to grab their bags and move out. Mr. Smith said he had a map to James' battalion area and would meet him after lunch. Mr. Smith turned to Tommy and asked where he would be. With a look of disappointment, Tommy answered that he was getting on a bus in a half an hour that would take him down to the airport for a flight to his new battalion located on the other coast. The Smith brothers realized this would be the last time they would see each other for some time and said their goodbyes.

James went to his barracks. His roommates told him the truck outside was from 1/X and could be used for their gear. James threw his bags on the truck and made his way to the bus where Corporal Wilson was standing. Corporal Wilson saw Private James Smith walking up. "Hey, Smith, congratulations," Wilson said, "Do you have all of your gear on that vehicle?" "Yes, corporal," James answered. "OK, climb aboard," Corporal Wilson said.

As James sat down, he saw his brother getting on another bus on the other side of the parking lot. Tommy had his head down as he climbed aboard the bus bound for the airport.

It was a short ride for James to his battalion area. Corporal Wilson pointed out several ranges, training areas, and hike routes along the way. When they arrived at the barracks, several Marines were waiting for the buses. Corporal Wilson took the six Marines assigned to his squad and led them to their rooms after they picked up their gear from the truck. James' name and the names of his roommates were already on the door when they arrived. Clean linen was folded neatly on their racks along with a folder labeled "Information Packet 1/X."

Corporal Wilson said they had an hour to unpack and make their racks. In an hour, he would meet them out front and take them to the chow hall to see their families. After the corporal left, James opened the information packet. It contained a base map; bus routes and schedules; and information about the gym, banks, barber shops, the chow hall, and other facilities.

An hour later, Corporal Wilson appeared outside. He formed up his squad and marched them about a quarter mile to a large parade deck. On it were several large tents with tables containing food and refreshments. Surrounding the parade deck were various tactical vehicles mounted with weapons systems. Several Marines were dressed in utilities with full field gear, and they had weapons ranging from the M-16 to an 81mm mortar to a .50 caliber machine gun. Corporal Wilson pointed out the battalion headquarters and chow hall. He said their families would be finished with chow shortly and would meet with them on the parade deck. He told the Marines they had 2 hours before evening

Sustaining the Transformation — 11

formation to look at the static displays, tour the battalion area, and show their families their barracks. Once Corporal Wilson dismissed the Marines, James found his parents at one of the demonstration sites. His father told him that the battalion commander spoke again at lunch, along with the sergeant major and the chaplain. Private James Smith spent the next 2 hours with his parents looking at the weapons demonstrations and touring the headquarters and barracks. That evening, James said goodbye to his parents, and he made his way to evening formation.

3 Months Later

Private First Class James Smith was promoted this morning. His entire squad congratulated him immediately following the company formation. During that same formation, Corporal Wilson received his sergeant chevrons. Private First Class Smith was excited and could not wait to tell his brother Tommy and his parents about his accomplishment.

James hadn't heard from his brother for some time. Tommy used to call often, but he never sounded happy. Since Tommy never had much to talk about, James would fill the conversation with stories about Sergeant Wilson, his platoon, and the Marines in his squad. When James asked Tommy what was wrong, Tommy would only reply that James was lucky.

James called to tell his brother about his promotion. Tommy didn't react well to the news. James asked Tommy when he'd be promoted to private first class. Tommy said he didn't know, that he had gotten into some trouble about a month ago and he wasn't sure what would happen. James tried, but he couldn't get Tommy to tell him what happened. Tommy would only say that he had made some bad choices since joining his unit, that he had made friends with some of the wrong people, and he had paid the price. Tommy told James that he was upset with what he had done and that he wanted to turn himself around and be the type of Marine they always dreamed of becoming. When James hung up, he felt bad about their conversation and he was concerned for his brother.

James then called his folks to pass on his good news. They were excited to hear about James' promotion. They told James about the letter they had received from his platoon commander stating what a fine job he was doing and his upcoming promotion. His parents said it had been some time since Tommy had called home, and they were starting to worry. They asked if James had heard from Tommy lately. James assured them that Tommy was okay and that they had recently spoken.

James hung up from talking to his parents. He felt a little down because he was worried about his brother, and he wondered what could have happened to him and how he could have gotten into trouble. Both of them had wanted to be Marines since they were kids and couldn't wait for the day they could wear the eagle, globe, and anchor. Now, only 3 months after arriving at his unit, Tommy wasn't hacking it. Although Private First Class Smith was bothered by the news of his brother, he had little time to waste. Sergeant Wilson had assigned him to teach a class on crossing linear danger areas during the squad patrolling exercise the next day. James was excited about the opportunity to teach his fellow squad members and proud that Sergeant Wilson had picked him to do it. He turned to his desk and the stack of class handouts and field manuals. He would spend the evening reviewing his handouts and creating a class outline that would make Sergeant Wilson proud.

(reverse blank)

Chapter 2

Understanding the Transformation

"I expect Marines to epitomize that which is good about our nation and to personify the ideals upon which it was founded. I do not intend for 'honor, courage, and commitment' to be just words; I expect them to frame the way that we live and act as Marines."[3]

—General C. C. Krulak

"The human heart is the starting point in all matters pertaining to war."[4]

—Frederick the Great

"These men are in the formative period of their lives, and officers owe it to them, their parents, and to the nation, that when discharged from the services they should be far better men physically, mentally, morally than when they were enlisted."[5]

—John A. Lejeune

Sustaining the Transformation

Honor, courage, commitment—these are our core values. They are values that ALL MARINES must inculcate and demonstrate in their every action. These values are our ethos. Weave this ethos through the very fabric of your being, and you earn the right to wear the title of United States Marine.

As a Corps, we provide two critical services for our nation: we make Marines and we win battles. Unless we "make Marines" correctly, we jeopardize our ability to "win battles" and, thus, our very existence. The Marines we make today will need this ethos of core values to win the battles of tomorrow. We must ensure that every Marine has been armed with the courage to confront tomorrow's confusing, chaotic battlespace. We must "issue" every Marine a true compass of personal honor and the commitment to forego interests of self for the interests of their comrades, their Corps, and their country.

On tomorrow's battlefield, Marines will be challenged to operate in an environment of peace, crisis, and war within a very short period of time. We have already experienced this on a small scale in Mogadishu, Somalia, with Marines providing humanitarian assistance on one block, dealing with a civil disturbance on the next, and on yet another block fully engaging in armed combat. This "three-block war" phenomenon promises to be commonplace in future conflicts. Tomorrow's battlefield will be technologically supercharged, ill-defined, and compounded by the confusion of the "three-block war's" characteristics. It will require rapid, more complex decisionmaking at lower levels and place greater stress on the individual Marine than ever before. Today, we are making the Marines of tomorrow, who will face the future battlefield and win; we are transforming our young Americans into Marines.

Why the Transformation

The first reason for the transformation was that we saw a change in the operating environment in which our Marines would be employed and we needed to prepare our young Marines for future battles. Decentralized operations, advanced technology, increasing weapons lethality, asymmetric threats, the mixing of combatants and noncombatants, and urban combat will be the way we fight vice the exception in the 21st century. To succeed in a changing operating environment, our Marines must be good decisionmakers. They must be trained to the highest standard. They must be self-confident. They must have absolute faith in the members of their unit. This is why we have instituted the Marine Corps Values Program for all Marines, and why we have enhanced the way we transform America's sons and daughters into United States Marines. We must ensure that our newest Marines fully understand and appreciate what the Marine Corps represents and that, by becoming members of the world's fighting elite, they uphold the sacred trust we have with our great nation and with each other. The transformation is designed specifically to contribute to the making of this kind of Marine.

The second reason for the transformation was derived from subtle changes in the norms and expectations of America's youth. The term generation X, often associated with a negative connotation, is the generation from which we will recruit the Marines who will be our future. Therefore, we must understand how this generation views the world and what motivates them. In 1994, we hired a team of psychologists to tell us about generation X. From them, we learned that young people today are looking for standards; they want to be held accountable. For the most part they don't mind following, but they can lead, and they want to lead. Most want to be part of something bigger than themselves. They want to be something special. Most believe in God. Many don't fully recognize it as such, but they want to have faith in something greater than themselves. These wants cause them to join gangs, fraternities, clubs, and other causes. These are also the same attributes and attitudes that offer the Marine Corps a tremendous opportunity. Generation X does not want to be babied. These young Americans are looking for a real challenge. They desperately want to be part of a winning team; they crave the stature associated with being one of the best. From them will come the Marines of the future—the warriors of the 21st century. The transformation gives them exactly what they want, and it also give us what we need.

However, transformation is not just a new block of instruction. It is not a new event introduced at recruit training. *Transformation is an ongoing, dynamic process.* It is a process that begins with an individual's first contact with a Marine recruiter and continues throughout a Marine's life. Transformation has five phases: recruitment, recruit training, cohesion, sustainment, and citizenship.

Transformation: Phase I

"I heartily wish we could raise men as fast as you equip ships."[6]
Lord St. Vincent

The first phase of the transformation process begins with our recruiters. They carefully screen the young people who come to our door seeking admittance. Those who have solid character, good moral standards, and personal values are those we embrace and validate, and we reinforce the values they hold. Those with undamaged characters, but who are among our society's many "empty vessels," we fill with the ideals and values they so desperately need and seek. We evaluate each candidate based on the whole person and decide on acceptance or rejection through an analysis of risk versus potential.

During recruitment, we make it clear who they are joining and what it is they are expected to become. The Marine recruiter is their mentor and launches their transformation. The recruiter introduces poolees to the concept of total fitness—body, mind, and spirit—in our improved delayed-entry program. Poolees are better prepared when they reach recruit training because they receive their first introduction to our core values, enhanced physical conditioning, knowledge of our history and traditions, and study guides that facilitate their transformation.

Sustaining the Transformation — 21

Transformation: Phase II

> *"We must remember that one man is much the same as another, and that he is best who is trained in the severest school."*[7]
>
> Thucydides

The second phase of transformation takes place during recruit training. During this phase, we prepare all Marines—male and female, those destined for combat arms, and those destined for combat service or combat service support—to fight on the nonlinear, chaotic battlefield of the future.

During the second phase, the drill instructor becomes the next person to transform the life of the young Marine. The drill instructor is still the backbone of the recruit training process, and he serves as a role model as recruits accelerate in their transformation. The drill instructor's role during the first 10 weeks of recruit training is unchanged, but in October of 1996, recruit training was lengthened to 12 weeks to accommodate an event we call the Crucible. While the event itself is new to recruit training, the concept of a crucible is not. FMFM 1-0, *Leading Marines* (to be reissued as MCWP 6-11), reminds us that "all Marines pass through the crucible of our entry level training. In that harsh and uncompromising forge, their steel is tempered to withstand the stresses of future challenges even more severe and testing."[8] This is the common bond of all Marines, shared by the Marines of tomorrow and the Marines of yesteryear.

During recruit training, the Crucible is the defining moment for a young Marine. *It will not be the hardest challenge Marines face in their entire lives but, for most, the Crucible will be the first time they reach the limits of their mental, physical, and emotional endurance. They will know that they are capable of much more than they previously believed.* They will know that they can exceed their own personal limitations through teamwork, perseverance, and courage. The Crucible, once experienced, will be a personal touchstone and will demonstrate for each and every recruit and candidate the limitless nature of what they can achieve individually and, more importantly, what they can accomplish when they work as a team.

The Crucible consists of 54 hours of intense, physically-demanding training, under conditions of sleep and food deprivation. During this time, recruits will be forged in the furnace of shared hardship and tough training that is the time-tried and battle-proven trademark of Marine recruit training. There will be night forced marches, a tough night infiltration movement, a combat resupply event, a casualty evacuation drill, and combat field firing. Any recruit who quits will not bear the title Marine.

Recruits will encounter unique obstacles, each bearing the name of a heroic Marine from our illustrious history, that can only be negotiated with teamwork. Once each obstacle is overcome, the drill instructor mentors the recruits, critiques their efforts, and retells the story of the individual for whom the obstacle was named, bringing to light how that individual exemplified our core values.

Sustaining the Transformation — 23

The Crucible is tough, but it is simply a visible manifestation of our values, our ethos. If we don't provide the right instruction and mind-set, the Crucible becomes just another rope and log obstacle course. Its true intent, which is teamwork, over and over again, teamwork and commitment to one's fellow Marine, is lost. It is the drill instructor's responsibility to be the pivotal role model, leader, and mentor of these young Marines, to show them how to function as a team, and to teach them to persevere.

The drill instructor's job is not over when his recruits complete the Crucible. The 12th week is known as transition week. It is literally the time when our newest members have the opportunity—and the responsibility—to increase their knowledge and confidence so that they are fully prepared for what lies ahead.

Much of the transformation process occurs during recruit training. But recruit training is only the second of five phases in the process.

Transformation: Phase III

> *"Consider your corps as your family; your commander as your father; your comrade as your brother; your inferior as a young relative. Then all will be happy and friendly and easy. Don't think of yourself, think of your comrades; they will think of you. Perish yourself, but save your comrades."*[9]
> General Mikhail Ivanovich Dragomirov

The third phase of the transformation process is the strengthening of the cohesion that was born during recruit training, the cohesion that binds Marines together. We define cohesion as the intense bonding of Marines, strengthened over time, resulting in absolute trust, subordination of self, an intuitive understanding of the collective actions of the unit, and appreciation for the importance of teamwork. To foster cohesion, we strive to form close-knit teams early, at the skill-producing schools. We try to keep these teams of Marines together through their first enlistment. By forming teams early, keeping the teams together, and assigning the teams to a unit, we enhance unit cohesion. This cohesion increases fighting power, provides positive peer pressure, and reinforces our core values as the team's collective sense of honor becomes dominant over self-interest. The teams train together, garrison together, deploy together, and fight together. We endeavor to send Marines together to units at the lowest level possible, and to keep them together as long as possible. However, this is not an easy task for our manpower managers, and we do not expect a 100 percent success rate. Many Marines will have to be assigned alone. Leaders receiving these Marines must ensure that they are properly sponsored, received, and coalesced into their units.

However, cohesion cannot simply be among peers. Of equal importance is the manner in which individual Marines and their teams identify with their units. The cohesion of a larger unit is the result of several teams of Marines joining for a common mission. All leaders must make unit cohesion one of their highest priorities and principal objectives. The more we reinforce the cohesion of our units, the stronger

Sustaining the Transformation — 25

our units will be and the easier it will be to reinforce individual core values through positive peer pressure, mentoring, and leadership.

Transformation: Phase IV

> *"Neither money nor machines can serve as a substitute for our fighting men. We cannot buy justice or freedom. We cannot manufacture them. And wanting them, we have got to be willing to fight for them—without any selfish thoughts of our own personal convenience. This is what we must ask, first of ourselves and then of our children."*[10]
>
> General David M. Shoup

The fourth phase of transformation is sustainment. Sustainment is continuous, and it will span all we do as Marines throughout our service. Our professional military education schools are designed to educate our leaders—our officers, staff NCOs, and NCOs—in "whole Marine" character development. Leaders in the operating forces and in the supporting establishment accomplish their missions in ways that support and reinforce our core values and foster team building. Leaders will manifest our core values and mentor their subordinates. We will live our ethos through a shared responsibility for all Marines that lasts until the day a Marine hangs up the uniform for the last time . . . and even longer.

Transformation: Phase V

> *"It's a funny thing, but, as years go by, I think you appreciate more and more what a great thing it was to be a U.S. Marine. I certainly can't say that I was happy every minute I was on active duty . . . People will tell me what a shame it was I had to go back in the service the second time, but now I'm kinda glad I did . . . Besides, I am a U.S. Marine and I'll be one till I die."*[11]
>
> Ted Williams (Hall of Fame baseball player and Marine Corps fighter pilot during World War II in Korea)

The fifth phase of transformation is citizenship. Beyond preparing young Marines to win in combat, what truly distinguishes our legacy to our nation are the citizens we produce—citizens transformed by their Marine experience and enriched by their internalization of our ethos, ideals, and values. As Marines, they have learned a nobler way of life, they are able to draw from their experiences, and they are prepared to be leaders within the Corps and within their communities and businesses. During the making of a Marine, our nation's most tangible benefit comes to fruition during the fifth phase, and that is citizenship. We produce citizens with our core values—the highest ideals in the American character—and place them in an environment where they are held accountable for those values. As Lieutenant General Victor H. Krulak wrote in his book, *First to Fight*, Marines "are masters of a form of unfailing alchemy which converts unoriented youths into proud, self-reliant stable citizens—citizens into whose hands the nation's affairs may safely be entrusted."[12]

Although our Corps has its share of heroic figures, in the minds of the American people our fame is collective—not individual. Ask the average American to name a famous soldier or sailor, and he will quickly respond with such names as Robert E. Lee, John Paul Jones, Douglas MacArthur, or George Patton. Ask them to name a famous Marine, and they will most likely draw a blank. Yet, to them, the word "Marine" is synonymous with honor, courage, and commitment—our core values. They expect them to rise above self-interest, and they expect them to lead. Their expectations of former Marines are the same as those they place on active and reserve Marines. When we "make Marines," we make Marines for life, we provide our nation with a legacy of productive citizens, transformed by their experiences while on active duty and enriched by their internalization of our ethos, ideals, and values.

Nearly 70 percent of all Marines are first-term enlistees. While a few will remain and provide our critical NCO and staff NCO leadership, most have other aspirations—yet unfulfilled dreams—and they will depart the active ranks upon completion of 4 years of faithful service. Approximately 20,000 Marines leave the Corps each year. Nonetheless, they will always be United States Marines. They earned that title during the Crucible and have lived up to those responsibilities ever since. The responsibility of being a Marine does not end when they leave our active ranks. In many respects, it only just begins. While they are no longer under the watchful eye of their company first sergeant and no longer subject to the Uniform Code of Military Justice, fellow Americans continue to judge our Marines, both past and present, by their actions and by the quality of their character for the rest of their lives.

When Marines depart the Corps, they will be in the ideal position to demonstrate that Marines reflect the values that Americans cherish most and hold in the highest regard—the values upon which this nation was founded, and which now guide us as we shoulder the responsibility of a world superpower. Be it a 4-year enlistment or a 35-year career, we all must sooner or later become former Marines. But we have every reason to take great pride in our service. We have done something that few Americans today ever consider doing—we have sacrificed our personal comfort and liberties for the health and needs of the nation. In return, we were imbued with time-tested values of honor, courage, and commitment that provide the foundation for personal success in any endeavor. These values serve as a moral compass as we return to school or join the workforce, and these values will make us leaders in our universities, workplaces, and communities.

Chapter 3

Cohesion

"Pride exists only among people who know each other well, who have esprit de corps, and company spirit. There is a necessity for an organization that renders unity possible by creating the real individuality of the company."[13]

—Ardant du Picq

"My first wish would be that my Military family, and the whole Army, should consider themselves as a band of brothers, willing and ready to die for each other."[14]

—General George Washington

Sustaining the Transformation — 31

Cohesion is the intense bonding of Marines, strengthened over time, that results in absolute trust. It is characterized by the subordination of self and an intuitive understanding of the collective actions of the unit and of the importance of teamwork, resulting in increased combat power. Cohesion is achieved by fostering positive peer pressure and reinforcing our core values to the point that our core values become dominant over self-interest.

A good example of this esprit is when the individual Marine risks his life to aid a fellow Marine or to accomplish the mission at hand. An example from our past includes the cohesion that bound Presley O'Bannon and his few Marines together during their march across 600 miles of scorching desert to stand triumphant at the shores of Derna. Another example is that of a trapped Marine division that bravely fought its way across the frozen wastes of Korea, through six communist divisions, to the sea. Cohesion provides Marines with supportive relationships that buffer stress and increases their ability to accomplish the mission or task. Strong unit cohesion results in increased combat power and the achievement of greater successes.

Dimensions of Cohesion

There are five dimensions of cohesion: individual morale, confidence in the unit's combat capability, confidence in unit leaders, horizontal cohesion, and vertical cohesion. In combination, these dimensions dramatically affect the capabilities of a unit.

Historically, the Corps has fostered individual morale, confidence in the unit's combat capability, and confidence in unit leaders. We understand the benefits attained through developing and maintaining high morale, and we have always stressed the technical and tactical proficiency of every Marine. Equally, our Corps has always emphasized the importance of developing solid, trustworthy leaders. Our reputation is built on the emphasis our forebearers put on these three dimensions of cohesion. The remaining two dimensions, horizontal and vertical cohesion, are also of equal importance to combat readiness, and this chapter focuses on these two dimensions of cohesion.

Individual Morale

As leaders, we must know our Marines and look out for their welfare. Leaders who understand that "morale, only morale, individual morale as a foundation under training and discipline, will bring victory"[15] are more likely to keep morale high among individual Marines. A high state of morale, in turn, enhances unit cohesion and combat effectiveness.

Confidence in the Unit's Combat Capability

Marines' confidence in their unit's combat capability is gained through unit training. The longer Marines serve and train together in a unit, the more effective they become and the more confident they are in their unit's capabilities. They know what their unit can do because they have worked together before. Keeping Marines together through unit cohesion is a combat multiplier. Rarely are battles lost by those who maintain confidence in their unit and in their fellow Marines. Success in battle can be directly attributed to a unit's overall confidence in its level of performance. Of course, the opposite also holds true; lack of cohesion, lack of confidence, and poor performance preordain a unit's failure. "If the history of military organizations proves anything, it is that those units that are told they are second-class will almost inevitably prove that they are second-class."[16]

Confidence in Unit Leaders

Confidence in unit leaders' abilities is earned as Marines spend time in the company of their seniors and learn to trust them. Leaders must earn the respect of their Marines, and doing so takes time. As Marines develop confidence, based on their prior achievements, in their units' ability to accomplish their assigned missions, they also develop confidence in their leaders as they work and train together. Major General John A. Lejeune believed that—

> The relation between officers and men should in no sense be that of superior and inferior nor that of master and servant, but rather that of teacher and scholar. In fact, it should partake of the nature of the relation between father and son, to the extent that officers, especially commanding officers, are responsible for the physical, mental, and moral welfare, as well as the discipline and military training of the young men under their command.[17]

Horizontal Cohesion

Why is horizontal cohesion important? Is it as important on the asymmetrical battlefield of today as it was in the island-hopping campaigns of World War II? The answer is yes! Horizontal cohesion, also known as peer bonding, takes place among peers. It is the building of a sense of trust and familiarity between individuals of the same rank or position. Sense of mission; teamwork; personnel stability; technical and tactical proficiency; trust, respect, and friendship are some elements that contribute to peer bonding.

An example of horizontal cohesion is the relationship between members of a fire team. Over time, each member develops a sense of trust in the other. This trust is born of several elements. The first is a common sense of mission, the act of placing personal goals aside to pursue the goals of the entire team. Other elements include teamwork and personnel stability. Teamwork is the result of mutual support provided by each member of the team. Teamwork is further enhanced by personnel stability, which promotes familiar and effective working relationships. Perhaps most important is the development of tactical and technical proficiency that continues to support and reinforce the trust and respect between the team members. When our young Marines are thrust deep into the chaotic battlespace, often operating in small teams, their will to fight and ultimately succeed will hinge upon their ability to fight as an effective, cohesive team.

Vertical Cohesion

Vertical cohesion is not new to our Corps; this dimension of cohesion involves the vertical relationship between subordinate and senior. Vertical cohesion is what draws peer groups into a cohesive unit, such as a battalion or squadron. It is, in part, the building of a mutual sense of trust and respect among individuals of different rank or position. Additionally, vertical cohesion is the sense of belonging that the squad or section maintains relative to its role in the battalion or squadron. Some characteristics of vertical cohesion include unit pride and history, leaders' concern for the Marines, leaders' example, trust and respect for leaders, and shared discomfort and danger.

An example of vertical cohesion is when many squads and sections come together to form a cohesive company. Each of these subordinate units plays a different role in the company; however, vertical cohesion draws them together in purpose and mutual support. This sense of unity has several elements. The first is a common sense of unit pride and history—pride not only in themselves as a unit, but also pride in those who have gone before them. The organizational memory of their past achievements drives the unit to still greater heights. Another element that contributes to vertical cohesion is the quality of leadership and the command climate in the unit. Vertical cohesion is stronger in units with effective, well-trained subordinate leaders. Leaders that show concern for their Marines and lead by example will earn the trust and respect of their subordinates. Another element of vertical cohesion includes shared discomfort and danger which can occur during shared training.

A historical example of vertical cohesion is the Scottish Rifles at the Battle of Neuve Chapelle, in March of 1915. Nine hundred men marched into battle; a scant 150 returned with only one surviving officer. Despite their casualties, the unit never faltered; they survived and endured because they were part of a family called a regiment. Their sense of worth, sense of individual honor, and their very being were bound up in the ethos of the Scottish Rifles. Individually, their lives were less important to them than the honor of their regiment. In the end, their sacrifice was not in vain. The British achieved both tactical and strategic victories during the battle. The Scots captured a salient that had been held by the Germans; a tactical victory. Their courage under fire so impressed the French that relations between the British Army and the French were much improved thereafter. Additionally, the tenacity of the Scots forced the Germans to commit their reserves to the battle, which relieved beleaguered French positions. Thus, the sacrifices of the Scottish Rifles also had profound strategic implications.

Mutual Support of Horizontal and Vertical Cohesion

Since the birth of our Corps, Marine units have evidenced horizontal and vertical cohesion to varying degrees and with varying success. However, it is vitally important that these

Sustaining the Transformation

two qualities be developed in combination with each other. Just as the strength of combined arms comes from the combined effects of two or more different arms that mutually support one another, the strength of horizontal and vertical cohesion derives from the combined effects and mutual support they provide each other.

Blending vertical cohesion and horizontal cohesion ensures a strong, universal sense of bonding and teamwork among various types of units. If vertical and horizontal cohesion are mutually supported, all these units will be composed of Marines who trust and respect each other. Each type of bond reinforces the other. A cohesive battalion that is comprised of cohesive companies which place the goals and interests of the battalion or company above those of their squad and/or section is an example of the blending of both vertical and horizontal cohesion.

The figure on page 38 depicts that to truly sustain the transformation, we must combine both the vertical cohesion axis and horizontal cohesion axis to achieve our goal of combat readiness. A unit capable of combining vertical and horizontal cohesion is far stronger than a unit which is strong in only a single axis.

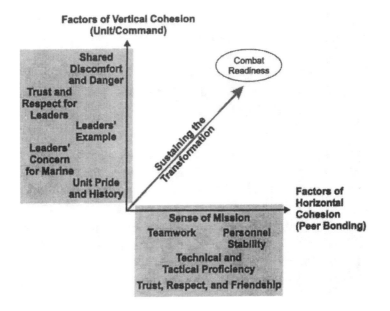

Chapter 4

Obstacles and Obstacle Reduction

"Natural hazards, however formidable, are inherently less dangerous and less uncertain than fighting hazards. All conditions are more calculable, all obstacles more surmountable, than those of human resistance. By reasoned calculation and preparation they can be overcome almost to timetable. While Napoleon was able to cross the Alps in 1800 'according to plan', the little fort of Bard could interfere seriously with the movement of his army as to endanger his whole plan."[18]

—Captain Sir Basil Liddell Hart

"Four brave men who do not know each other will not dare to attack a lion. Four less brave, but knowing each other well, sure of their reliability and consequently of mutual aid, will attack resolutely. There is the science of the organization of armies in a nutshell."[19]

—Colonel Ardant du Picq

Obstacles to sustainment vary from unit to unit and, therefore, are difficult to define for the entire Corps. Generally, an obstacle is anything that detracts from a unit's ability to establish a productive environment for its Marines. To provide a productive environment, a command must commit itself to identifying its obstacles and determining how they can be overcome.

Section I. Obstacles

Critical Factors Affecting Sustainment

Once Marines arrive at their new units, they begin a critical period wherein several opportunities exist for reinforcement or disillusionment. These opportunities will influence their decisions at a number of decision points and they will ask themselves, "Do I want to be part of this organization?" Their response will be one of two paths: they will either become "self-sustaining," headed toward successful enlistments and aiding others in sustainment, or they will become "at-risk," headed for first-term, non-expiration of active service (EAS) attrition. The figure on page 42 illustrates how each of the individual decision points can be opportunities to create either a "self-sustaining" Marine or an "at-risk" Marine.

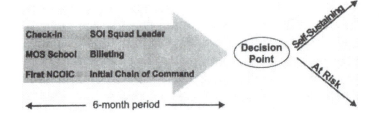

Check-In
Have Marines been assigned and met their mentors during their first exposure to the fleet? Is the mentor a positive influence and representative of the unit's values and culture? Have Marines become "check-in orphans," victims of consolidated administrative sections, with little guidance and leadership?

SOI Squad Leader
Is the squad leader a solid mentor or an obvious deviation from the polished NCO or staff NCO that Marines sought to emulate in boot camp?

MOS School
Is cohesion maintained in MOS schools? Have the schools embraced values training as a continuation of the transformation?

Billeting
Are Marines given adequate billeting and welcomed aboard? Have Marines been given any available empty barracks space? How does the unit receive Marines who arrive after normal duty hours?

First NCO in Charge (NCOIC)
Does the NCOIC make a good impression on the new Marines and take care of them? Does the NCOIC know how to establish goals and uphold standards? Are Marines made to feel as though they are part of the larger team, so they sense the necessary vertical cohesion? Are the standards the Marines are taught in boot camp universally enforced?

Initial Chain of Command
Does a positive chain of command exist? Does the climate support the establishment of goals and uphold standards for the individual and the unit? Is routine counseling and leadership training conducted? Does a strong sense of unit pride and history exist?

Sustaining the Transformation

Quadrant Model

The quadrant model categorizes the obstacles that individuals or units encounter in sustaining the transformation. The model uses two methods.

In the first method, obstacles are categorized as either reality-based or perception-based. Reality-based obstacles must be overcome through policy changes or changes in command directives. Perception-based obstacles can typically be overcome through education to correct misinformation or prejudice.

In the second method, obstacles are categorized as either unit-generated or as being systemic to our Corps. Obstacles encountered by a specific unit can be corrected through good leadership at the local level. Obstacles systemic to our Corps must be addressed by both Headquarters, Marine Corps and by local commanders.

Categorizing obstacles in this way places them into four separate quadrants, as illustrated in the following figure.

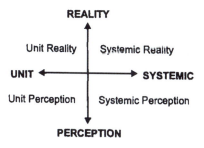

Reality-Based Unit Obstacles

Reality-based unit obstacles are the result of internal friction encountered by and attributed to individual units. These obstacles may not be widespread throughout the Corps, but, nonetheless, they are significant to the units that encounter them. Often these obstacles are unit-imposed and can be overcome through good leadership. The following text identifies some reality-based unit obstacles; although these examples are not inclusive, they are the most common.

- Insufficient Leadership Training. Some units become overwhelmed by inspector general (IG) inspections, the Marine Corps Combat Readiness Evaluation System (MCCRES), field supply and maintenance analysis office (FSMAO) visits, and maintenance-related reviews. If they focus on these issues alone, they lose sight of the value of leadership training. Although leadership training is time-intensive, we must ensure adequate training for both current and future NCOs, staff NCOs, and junior officers.
- Insufficient Contact. Commands often fail to monitor the progress of Marines assigned to temporary duty away from their command. Frequently, these Marines return to their units feeling isolated from their Marine family.
- Identification with Peers Vice Unit. When there is a breakdown of vertical cohesion, Marines only identify with their peers and not with their units. Marines in a group are loyal only to those Marines within the immediate group.

- Individual Impact on Unit Success. Some Marines fail to make the connection between group objectives and command mission. Failing to understand the impact they have on the operation of the unit causes them to disassociate from the unit.

- Leadership Turnover. Some leadership billets experience a high degree of turnover, which degrades the leaders' ability to foster effective working relationships and loyalties. Essential leadership principles such as "knowing your Marines" take time to achieve.

- Marine Corps Standards. As Marines witness deviations from, and a lack of adherence to, required standards, their opinions of both the command and the standards suffer. Lowering or overlooking standards affects the sustainment process by reducing Marines' expectations of the Corps and reducing their sense of accomplishment.

- Operational Tempo. Commands focus time and effort on training for upcoming deployments, exercises, and operations. This focus can override efforts to develop subordinate Marines as leaders. Due to time constraints, missions are often assigned to the most experienced Marines so "it is done right the first time." This assignment policy does not empower our junior Marines to take responsibility, to make errors, and to learn from them. Developing junior leadership is a fundamental factor in sustaining the transformation.

- Insufficient Challenges. Many Marines joined the Corps, in part, to be challenged to the fullest extent of their capabilities. They received challenges throughout their recruit training and their follow-on schools.

Disillusionment occurs if their units have low individual and unit expectations.
- Ineffective Mentors. Marines emulate the role models within their unit. Without a proper mentor, a Marine may choose a negative role model and become an "at-risk" Marine. Commanders must focus on training newly joined Marines, ensuring solid leadership, imparting productive mentoring, and providing positive examples.
- Insufficient Discipline. Discipline is degraded when commands relax standards, whether traditional customs or published regulations. Marines must recognize that they are all responsible for and capable of enforcing good discipline.

Perception-Based Unit Obstacles

Perception-based unit obstacles are the result of unit-held perceptions. They evolve from locally-held prejudices and lack of education. Educating our Corps on the transformation process will diminish the misconceptions of the transformation and diminish unit perception problems. These misconceptions can include—
- Labeling. The labeling of Marines as "cohesion" Marines or "crucible" Marines adds to the perception of differences among Marines. These perceptions or prejudices, often negative, do not account for individual abilities, and they negatively affect how Marines are accepted into a unit. This labeling is similar to the labeling that occurred during the introduction of

Sustaining the Transformation — 47

maneuver warfare, where Marines were labeled as either "maneuverists" or "attritionists." This resulted in animosity and reduced the initial effectiveness of the concept of maneuver warfare.

- "Broken" Marines. Many of our junior Marines are "broken" due to dysfunctional societal values. Our recruiting processes are specifically geared to ensure this is not the case. However, many of our young Marines are "empty vessels" who seek guidance and values from our Corps. While this appears to be an obstacle, it is actually an opportunity.
- Cohesion Team Perceptions. The perception is that, if one Marine within a cohesion team is substandard, then the group will take on these negative attributes as well.
- Counseling. Counseling more often results from negative behavior than from continuous performance appraisal. Commands must recognize the utility of counseling for situations other than promotions, pro/con marking, or nonjudicial punishment (NJP).

Reality-Based Systemic Obstacles

Reality-based systemic obstacles are prevalent throughout the Marine Corps and are caused by factors outside the control of small units. Additionally, these obstacles are not due to misconceptions or misunderstandings; they are based on fact. The following are examples of common, reality-based systemic obstacles:

- Mundane, Repetitive Daily Routines. Marines often feel overwhelmed when facing months of performing the same duty in the same manner. Repetition of duty causes a lack of job satisfaction.
- Separate Billeting That Degrades Unit Cohesion. Commands still have difficulties ensuring their Marines are billeted together. Dorm-style rooms are sometimes filled on a space-available basis, with little regard for parent command or unit integrity.

Perception-Based Systemic Obstacles

Perception-based systemic obstacles are prevalent throughout the Marine Corps. They are caused by Corps-wide misconceptions or misunderstandings. These misconceptions can include, but are not limited to, the following examples:

- Promotions. Cutting scores affect promotions, not just time in service. Marines perceive that promotions will be granted unless a Marine has been the subject of disciplinary action. These perceptions are reinforced when the only Marines who do not receive their commander's recommendations for promotion are those with habitual conduct problems.
- The Crucible. Throughout entry-level training, recruits are told that the Crucible will be the toughest event that they will endure. But this event is a stepping stone to the many other difficult challenges they

Sustaining the Transformation — 49

will face in their lives. Recruits should not be told that the Crucible is the most difficult challenge they will face. They should be told that it is the most strenuous challenge they will be required to meet up to that point in their Marine Corps experience, and that it will prepare them to meet future, even more difficult challenges that they will encounter upon joining their operational units.

- Nonjudicial Punishment. Marines fail to recognize or use methods other than NJP as valid forms of discipline. NJP is not the only form of discipline available to subordinate commanders. NCOs can use counseling or proper corrective action to rectify problems.

Section II. Obstacle Reduction

The commander is responsible for creating a climate that allows junior leaders to effectively apply Marine Corps leadership principles. As Marines enter their unit for the first time, they closely observe the unit, and they quickly assess the actions and practices of their leaders and their peers. Experience has taught us that if a Marine feels there are too many obstacles to allow him to integrate into the unit, he will fail. Thus it is incumbent upon us to reduce these obstacles and foster esprit de corps. The following paragraphs discuss some obstacle reduction methods.

Accepting Constraints and Reality

Marines take pride in being able to meet challenges and achieve success. Success is founded on a leader's ability to identify an obstacle, recognize and accept the constraints, and find a workable solution. Accepting the constraints is a key factor. All units encounter the reality of operational tempo and manpower shortfalls. Limits of time, money, manpower, and other external influences will always exist. Accepting these realities as constraints, instead of obstacles, enables a leader to focus on the actual obstacle at hand. Once obstacles are properly identified, a command can begin to identify means to overcome them. For example, commands that view manpower shortages as an obstacle must focus their efforts on filling vacancies rather than trying to more effectively use the Marines they have on hand.

Maintaining a Leadership Role

Marine Corps history is replete with examples of Marines who have overcome great odds to achieve success. These success stories have a common feature: initiative and ingenuity exercised by leaders at all levels. Our ability to overcome obstacles to sustaining the transformation depends on leaders who can use leadership principles to reduce obstacles.

Our junior leaders determine the obstacles that a command focuses on. Our small-unit leaders conduct the tasks, complete the missions, and ensure unit effectiveness for the

Sustaining the Transformation — 51

command. Their influence and impact on their subordinates' growth as future leaders determine a unit's success in sustaining the transformation. Our small-unit leaders, the "strategic corporals" of tomorrow, should be the Corps' primary focus to ensure success, both on and off the battlefield. To develop and employ effective junior leaders and small-unit leaders, our efforts must go beyond only training to attain tactical and technical proficiency. We must also focus on the leadership traits of our leaders:

- Dependability. The certainty of proper performance of duty.
- Bearing. Creating a favorable impression in carriage, appearance, and personal conduct at all times.
- Courage. The mental quality that recognizes fear of danger or criticism, but enables a man to proceed in the face of it with calmness and firmness.
- Decisiveness. Ability to make decisions promptly and to announce them in a clear, forceful manner.
- Endurance. The mental and physical stamina measured by the ability to withstand pain, fatigue, stress, and hardship.
- Enthusiasm. The display of sincere interest and exuberance in the performance of duty.
- Initiative. Taking action in the absence of orders.
- Integrity. Uprightness of character and soundness of moral principles. Integrity includes the qualities of truthfulness and honesty.
- Judgment. The ability to weigh facts and possible solutions on which to base sound decisions.

- Justice. Giving reward and punishment according to merits of the case in question. The ability to administer a system of rewards and punishments impartially and consistently.
- Knowledge. The range of one's information, including professional knowledge and an understanding of your Marines.
- Tact. The ability to deal with others without creating offense.
- Unselfishness. Avoidance of providing for one's own comfort and personal advancement at the expense of others.
- Loyalty. The quality of faithfulness to country; the Corps; the unit; and to one's seniors, subordinates, and peers.

Understanding Leadership Principles

As is written in Ecclesiastes, "There is no new thing under the sun."[20] With leadership as a focus, we can begin to examine how we can better prepare our young Marines to overcome obstacles. To sustain the transformation and create effective units, we must rely on a command's ability to emphasize and reinforce the tried-and-true principles of leadership:

- Know yourself and seek self-improvement.
- Be technically and tactically proficient.
- Develop a sense of responsibility among your subordinates.

Sustaining the Transformation

- Make sound and timely decisions.
- Set the example.
- Know your Marines and look out for their welfare.
- Keep your Marines informed.
- Seek responsibility.
- Take responsibility for your actions.
- Ensure assigned tasks are understood, supervised, and accomplished.
- Train your Marines as a team.
- Employ your command in accordance with its capabilities.

Everyone in the Corps either knows or remembers some of these principles, but many do not consistently and universally apply them. Obstacles to sustainment are obstacles to the application of our leadership principles.

Interacting with Schools

The benefits of interaction between commands and schools cannot be understated. Any effort commands can make toward easing the transition from schools to units will better prepare Marines to meet upcoming challenges.

Attending Unit-Level Corporal Courses

Upon promotion to corporal, some Marines understand their new grade and responsibilities by their observations of the corporals with whom they have served. Commands have an opportunity and responsibility to develop NCOs as leaders to ensure they are prepared to take on leadership challenges. Many units have implemented a 2-day corporal's course conducted by the command's staff NCOs. Though the course can be tailored to the unit's requirements, guidance in such areas as professional relations with subordinates, the NCO's role in sustaining the transformation, counseling, core values, mentoring, and applying leadership principles provide a sound starting point. This course must emphasize to newly promoted corporals that promotion to their new grade not only places them in charge of those in their unit, but also in charge of all Marines of lesser grade.

Encouraging Professional Military Education

Enlisted professional military education is another tool provided by the Corps to develop Marine leaders. While not mandatory for promotion, the long-term benefits of formal education for Marines and their unit outweigh the short-term loss of the individual.

Briefing New Joins

A new join briefing is an opportunity for the command to welcome aboard its new Marines and to provide some insight into the unit itself. Understanding the origin of unit traditions and history can initiate a sense of belonging and unit pride. This briefing should also ensure that Marines have a clear understanding of their new chain of command and how subordinate units fit within senior units.

Maintaining Bachelor Enlisted Quarters

The Commandant's bachelor enlisted quarters campaign plan is dedicated to providing Marines with living conditions that allow them to continue to develop as Marines. Marines' quarters should also foster unit integrity.

Providing Mentors

A Marine's attitudes, ethics, and traits frequently conform to those displayed by the role models provided by their unit. Commanders must ensure that the unit provides positive, quality mentors. Mentors should be assigned to Marines as they check-in.

Educating Leaders

Recent changes to recruit training and the SOI have led to many misconceptions, one being that training is not as good or as tough as it used to be. These misconceptions cause negative attitudes and lowered expectations.

To dispel these misconceptions, former drill instructors and recruiters in the command can provide current and accurate information. Accurate information enables Marines to recognize that while the training has changed and new terms are used, our entry-level training has the same focus—we still make Marines.

Drawing on External Resources

Sharing our successes in overcoming obstacles allows leaders to draw on the experience of others who have succeeded in overcoming the same obstacles and to tailor their solutions accordingly. We must provide a forum in which leaders can share their solutions.

Utilizing the World Wide Web

The Marine Corps home page (www.usmc.mil) provides an accessible location for storing and retrieving information. The site includes copies of ALMARs and speeches by the Commandant. Users can provide input and exchange ideas concerning sustaining the transformation.

Chapter 5

Universal Methods for Sustaining the Transformation

"The best tactical results [are obtained] from those dispositions and methods which link the power of one man to that of another. Men who feel strange with their unit, having been carelessly received by it, and indifferently handled, will rarely, if ever, fight strongly and courageously. But if treated with common decency and respect, they will perform like men."[21]

—Brigadier General S. L. A. Marshall

Sustaining the Transformation — 59

There are thousands of ways to sustain the transformation. Many of the methods discussed in this publication are being used in the operating forces with great success. The following figure highlights some of the opportunities leaders can use to sustain the transformation. This chapter discusses these opportunities, but they by no means can be applied to every unit. Instead, they should serve as a reminder to leaders and be implemented wherever practicable.

1 YEAR
- Deployment
- Family Day
- 6-month Recognition
- Unit Training and Exercises
- Unit Events
- Battle Anniversary
- 1-month Recognition
- In-Briefs
- Graduation and Unit Reception
- Command Involvement

Command Involvement

ALMAR 454/96 states that the unit cohesion process "provides an opportunity for small unit leaders to be matched to their teams and provide leadership mentoring at the earliest possible opportunity."[22] The Commandant further states, "I expect small unit leaders to contact their teams of Marines before they graduate from SOI."[23] With that guidance, the sooner a unit can establish contact with incoming Marines the better. If possible, contact should be made at the SOI or the MOS school. As highlighted by Private John Smith's experience in chapter 1, "The Difference," a little effort can go a long way in ensuring a smooth transition for a new Marine. For example, one battalion commander phrased his commander's intent for welcoming a group of Marines after graduation from SOI as, "NCOs will participate in ITB training in order to facilitate unit cohesion, complete squad leaders' notebooks, determine any personal problems, and begin the transition to the battalion with an emphasis on battalion history, traditions, and combat SOPs."

The following paragraphs identify ways units can include their Marines who are undergoing MOS school training.

- Interaction with MOS Schools. The receiving unit coordinates with the MOS school to send squad leaders to observe training, meet their new Marines, and provide unit information.
- Command Liaison. If squad leader interaction is not possible for every unit, a command liaison will suffice. The liaison provides new Marines reporting to the unit with the unit's history, schedules, billeting, etc.
- Unit History Brief. The unit history brief provides new Marines with vertical cohesion at the earliest stages. A sense of pride develops as these young Marines realize they are becoming part of a rich, valiant legacy.

- Schedule and/or Deployment Brief. Many young Marines look forward to their deployment overseas. Unit schedules and deployment briefs are motivators for Marines and also assist them in mentally preparing for the future.

Graduation and/or Unit Reception

Command involvement at the SOI or MOS school graduation can also be beneficial. If unit leaders participate in the ceremony, graduation becomes an opportunity to initiate vertical cohesion with their Marines. The following paragraphs discuss other ways to use graduation and receptions to foster vertical cohesion. These should be executed expeditiously to ensure a seamless transition into the unit.

- Unit Reception. If possible, after graduation, the new Marines, and their gear, should be transported to the unit area by their new unit. The new squad leaders who have participated in training with these Marines can guide them through the check-in process. Upon arrival at their new unit, the new Marines should be welcomed to the unit by the commanding officer or sergeant major. The new Marines and their families can participate in a command-sponsored meal at the chow hall. Families may tour the unit area and billeting. Some units conduct static displays of various weapon systems and equipment to educate the families. These new Marines will also be guided through their administrative and logistical in-processing in an

efficient manner. This is a team effort that will require support from the entire unit.
- Unit Information Packet. Unit information packets ease the transition of Marines into their new units and provide answers to the many questions that result from relocating to a new environment. The packet also should include information on the unit's history, traditions, and future deployment schedules.
- Hometown News Releases. Hometown news releases assist in developing vertical cohesion. At a minimum, a news release should address the Marine by name and rank, identify his unit, and identify his accomplishments. For example, "PFC John Smith, having completed 4 months of intense training, has earned the privilege of joining 1/X, a highly decorated unit with a proud Marine Corps history. PFC John Smith will be a welcome addition to this proud unit."
- Command Letter to Families. Many families will not be able to attend the graduation or unit reception. A command letter may be the best way to ensure that all families are contacted. This letter should welcome the extended family and ensure them that their family member will be cared for.
- Assignment of a Mentor or a Sponsor. Upon arrival to a unit, Marines must be assigned a mentor who can assimilate them into the unit. The mentor can enhance both vertical and horizontal cohesion.

In-Briefs

Many units will receive small numbers of individuals and therefore cannot conduct a detailed unit reception. In this case, units must establish in-briefs that are conducted at regular periods in order to reach new Marines shortly after entering the unit.

One-Month Recognition

One month after Marines arrive at a unit, the command should recognize their contribution to the unit. This recognition increases Marines' vertical cohesion to the unit and command. Units can do this by giving awards to the most deserving Marines, such as a meritorious mast or a nonstandard, unit-specific award. Examples of nonstandard unit awards might be unit coins or T-shirts. This is another opportunity to send a command letter home in order to reinforce the positive behavior exhibited by the new Marines during that crucial first month period.

Battle Anniversary

Unit commanders should take the time to recognize the anniversary of a significant event or battle in which the unit participated. A good unit history program, complete with recognition of battles won, accolades earned, and sacrifices made, can also increase vertical cohesion.

Unit Events

- Sports Tournament and/or Field Day. Unit sporting events are time-proven methods that develop both horizontal and vertical cohesion.
- Unit Special Orders. Mentioning a unique and important contribution of a Marine or a unit of Marines at a unit formation provides visible recognition of the accomplishment on behalf of a unit's mission. Unit special orders are read at formations by the unit's commanding officer, executive officer, adjutant, or sergeant major.
- Marine Corps Birthday Ball. Because the Marine Corps Birthday Ball is rich with tradition, it is a perfect opportunity to build vertical cohesion. Commanders must ensure that the birthday ball is an affordable and enjoyable event filled with honor, history, and tradition.
- Marine's Birthday. Recognition of a Marine's birthday is another way to reinforce vertical cohesion at the small-unit level. The acknowledgement of this significant day is another example of the leadership principle "know your Marines."
- Unit Defining Moment. The Crucible provides the first defining moment in a Marine's career. Units should pick other events when they were stressed and tested as an entire unit. Following this challenge, while the unit still shares a sense of accomplishment, is an opportune time for a commander to praise his Marines.

- Personal Correspondence. Commanders should pen a short note to Marines to recognize significant accomplishments or milestones in their Marines' careers. Congratulations or expressions of sympathy are particularly important.
- Unit Symbol, Mascot, Logo, or Motto. Many units use a unit symbol, mascot, logo, or motto to give Marines a sense of belonging. These symbols make Marines feel like they are part of a larger and unique entity. This enables them to identify with the unit and aids in developing both horizontal and vertical cohesion.

Unit Training and Exercises

Unit training and exercises are often the best ways to develop horizontal cohesion. The interaction, close living quarters, and shared hardship of these exercises often bring Marines and units together. Once again, unit training and exercises should be either initiated or followed up by a command letter home and a hometown news release.

Six-Month Recognition

The 6-month recognition is similar to 1-month recognition; however, this is the last time that new Marines will be identified or addressed individually in this manner. After 6 months, they should have participated in exercises and operations and shared hardships and other experiences with the unit. A 6-month recognition can include events used during the 1-month recognition. It can also include, but is not limited to, the following recognitions:

- Meritorious Promotion. A meritorious promotion is an opportunity to recognize those new Marines who have excelled since their arrival.
- Command Logbook. During this ceremony, a battalion logbook should be on hand. This book would have inscribed the names of all the Marines who have belonged to that battalion. Each new Marine having honorably served with the unit for at least 6-months would sign the book.

Family Day

Nearly 50 percent of the active duty force is married. A family day serves as a fun-filled event for spouses and families as well as an informational brief. The command could use this opportunity to educate and prepare families for upcoming deployments.

Deployment

Deployment is what all the hard work has been for. A command letter and hometown news release are once again appropriate for this event.

Chapter 6

Endstate

"A spirit of comradeship and brotherhood in arms came into being in the training camps and on the battlefields. This spirit is too fine a thing to be allowed to die. It must be fostered and kept alive and made the moving force in all Marine organizations."[24]

—Major General John A. Lejeune

Sustaining the Transformation — 69

According to ALMAR 454/96, the transformation will produce "Marines fully prepared to fight on the 'mission depth' battlefield of the future and whose day-to-day performance reflects the high standard of the Marine Corps and the ideals of the nation it serves."[25] It will ultimately improve the effectiveness and efficiency of our Corps. Marine units, whether operating in a foreign land or at our home bases, are tasked with many and varied daily missions. In addition to these daily missions, they are regularly tasked to respond to situations requiring flexibility and adaptability. The ability of the unit to respond to these situations effectively is directly related to the abilities of the leaders and individual Marines in a unit and the unit's ability to work as a team. The more cohesive the unit and the more capable the individual Marines, the more flexible, adaptive, and successful will be the Corps.

Transformation will help us live up to the responsibility of returning better citizens to the nation. By instilling the values that we have always held true, we develop Marines who are capable of being solid and contributing citizens.

The foundation for the transformation was laid in recruiters' offices all across America, in the squad bays of our recruit depots, and at our formal, entry-level schools. As depicted in the figure on page 70, it is only a foundation, one upon which the Marine Corps must build. There are four pillars built on this foundation, four pillars upon which the transformation rests. These four pillars are education, NCO development, ownership and acceptance, and establishment and maintenance of standards.

We must continue to educate the Corps about the transformation process. Leaders of Marines must understand the process that developed their Marines. Armed with this knowledge, these leaders will understand the benefits gained through the transformation process and the true capabilities of their Marines.

Our NCOs are the key to sustaining the transformation. We must ensure we select the best to be NCOs and continue to train them to sustain the values and warfighting ethos of our Corps.

Every NCO, staff NCO, and officer must personally accept the mission to sustain the transformation of the Marines in their charge and those Marines they encounter throughout

Sustaining the Transformation

their daily routine. Every Marine must take personal ownership of the transformation.

As Marines, we will always strive to be the best, and we must continue to set the bar high in order to challenge our young men and women. Our young Marines expect to be held to the same high standards that they learned about in the recruiters' offices and that we established during recruit training; and they deserve nothing less.

These four pillars are crucial to the transformation and must remain strong for years to come. Maintaining the strength of each pillar is the responsibility of every Marine. On these pillars rests the weight of the future of our Marine Corps.

(reverse blank)

Definitions

cohesion—The intense bonding of Marines, strengthened over time, resulting in absolute trust. It is characterized by subordination of self and an intuitive understanding of the collective actions of the unit and of the importance of teamwork, resulting in increased combat power. Cohesion is achieved by fostering positive peer pressure and reinforcing our core values to the point that our Corps values become dominant over self-interest. It is comprised of team integrity and synchronization. Unit cohesion is part of the transformation process that will guarantee the Corps a rich legacy: Marines fully prepared to fight on the three-block war of the future and whose day-to-day performance reflects the high standard of the Marine Corps and the ideals of the nation it serves.

cohesion team—Marines of the same MOS grouped together at boot camp with the intention of keeping them together through their first enlistment. In ALMAR 454/96, commanders are directed to assign these teams of Marines to the smallest unit possible, optimally to the same squad. If assignment to the same squad is not possible, then assignment should be made to the same platoon or company.

Crucible—The Crucible is an event designed to help Marines prepare for battles through the inculcation of confidence, core values, and esprit de corps. The Crucible is the centerpiece of the recruit training phase of the transformation. It is a 3-day training event that has been added to the end of basic recruit training. It is designed specifically to make Marines better warriors. The events focus on two areas—shared hardship and teamwork.

horizontal cohesion—The horizontal bonding (also known as peer bonding) that takes place among peers. It is the building of a sense of trust and familiarity among individuals of the same rank or position. Some elements that contribute to horizontal bonding include sense of mission, technical and tactical proficiency, lack of personnel turbulence, teamwork, trust, respect, and friendship.

Marine Corps Values Program—The coordinated, integrated effort to enhance the transformation of a recruit into a Marine through a rigorous education in, and reaffirmation of, Marine Corps values. Its goal is to produce Marines who are warriors of integrity and character as well as exemplary citizens and who will act honorably and intelligently, in every situation and at every level of responsibility. There are three phases to the Marine Corps Values Program:

   a. Phase I. Initial Entry-Level Training—Every Marine, enlisted and officer, is instructed in Marine Corps values during entry-level training. The preponderance of the training occurs at the Marine Corps recruit depots for enlisted Marines and at Officer Candidates School and The Basic School for officers.

   b. Phase II. Reinforcement Education—The lessons of entry-level training are reinforced in Marine combat training at the School of Infantry for all enlisted Marines. Reinforcement training is also presented in

MOS schools for both enlisted Marines and officers. Core values education continues at every professional school that a Marine attends, from the Sergeant's Course through the Marine Corps War College. Additionally, gatherings of Marine leaders, such as the General Officers Symposium, Commanders' Courses, and Sergeants Major/Master Gunnery Sergeant Symposium, include discussions concerning values.

c. Phase III. Sustainment Education—Sustainment education not only involves formal presentations of course material, but also encompasses awareness of the importance that practicing core values has in each Marine's day-to-day life. Marines should be able to see core values demonstrated in the daily course of events by leaders at all levels, from squad to force commander. Honor, courage, and commitment must be a way of life in garrison and in the field, on and off duty.

sustainment—The fourth and most critical phase of both the transformation and the Marine Corps Values Program. Sustainment is the responsibility of unit leaders to maintain and build upon the values and warrior spirit built by formal schools and entry-level training.

synchronization—The process of aligning unit deployment schedules and the assignment of teams in order to allow the teams to remain in their assigned unit for the duration of their first enlistment. Synchronization works within the known constraints of the usable contract length of a first-term Marine and the dates of deployment to match the available personnel resources to the deployment in a manner that:

- Fulfills forward presence requirements.
- Fits deployments into the 42-month personnel cycle of a Marine.
- Enables structured progressive training with units being fully staffed 8-16 months prior to deployments.

team integrity—The forming of teams early in the entry-level pipeline, keeping the teams together, and then assigning the Marines, as a team, to a unit. The intent is that these teams will train together, garrison together, deploy together, and fight together and that commanders should take all steps necessary to ensure that Marines remain in their original units for as long as possible. Team integrity provides a means for ensuring that small groups of Marines move together from the Crucible through the MOS-producing schools and to operational units with their Marine ethos intact.

transformation—Transformation is the ongoing, dynamic process that begins with the prospective Marine's first contact with the Marine recruiter and continues through the Marine's entire life. It has five phases:

Phase I. Recruiting
Phase II. Recruit Training
Phase III. Cohesion
Phase IV. Sustainment
Phase V. Citizenship

vertical cohesion—This dimension of cohesion involves the relationship between subordinate and senior. It draws peer groups into a cohesive unit. This is, in part, the building of a mutual sense of trust and respect among individuals of different rank or position. More than this, however, it is the sense of belonging that the squad or section maintains for its role in the battalion or squadron. Some characteristics of vertical cohesion that contribute to military effectiveness are unit tradition and history, leaders' concern for the men, leaders' examples, trust and respect for leaders, and sharing of adversity and danger.

(reverse blank)

Notes

1. William Shakespeare, quoted in Robert Debs Heinl, Jr., Colonel, USMC, Retired, *Dictionary of Military and Naval Quotations* (Annapolis, MD: United States Naval Institute, 1966) p. 106.

2. General John A. Lejeune, quoted in Heinl, p. 172.

3. General C. C. Krulak, *Commandant's Planning Guidance* (Washington, D.C.: Headquarters, United States Marine Corps, 1995) p. 23.

4. Frederick the Great, quoted in MCRP 6-11B (with change 1), *Marine Corps Values: A User's Guide for Discussion Leaders* (Washington, D.C.: Headquarters, United States Marine Corps, 1998) p. 21-25.

5. General John A. Lejeune, quoted in MCRP 6-11B, p. 20-1.

6. Lord St. Vincent, letter to Lord Keith, 5 April 1803, p. 268.

7. Thucydides, *History of the Peloponnesian Wars*, quoted in Heinl, p. 328.

8. FMFM 1-0, *Leading Marines* (Washington, D.C.: Headquarters, United States Marine Corps, 1995) p. 31.

9. General Mikhail Ivanovich Dragomirov, *Notes for Soldiers*, quoted in Heinl, p. 106.

10. Extract from a speech given by General David M. Shoup, USMC, to the Defense Orientation Conferences Association (Washington, D.C., 28 September 1961).

11. Ted Williams, quoted in General C. C. Krulak, "The Former Marine: Transformation Phase 4B," *Marines* (October 1998) p. 2.

12. Ibid., quoting Lieutenant General Victor H. Krulak, *First to Fight: An Inside View of the U.S. Marine Corps* (Annapolis, MD: Naval Institute Press, 1984).

13. Ardant du Picq, Battle Studies, quoted in Robert A. Fitton, ed., *Leadership: Quotations from the Military Tradition* (Boulder, CO: Westview Press, 1990) p. 41.

14. General George Washington, 21 October 1798, letter to Henry Knox, quoted in Peter G. Tsouras, *Warriors' Words: A Quotation Book: From Sesostris III to Schwarzkopf, 1871 BC to AD 1991* (London: Cassell Arms and Armour Press, 1992) p. 82.

15. Sir William Slim, to the officers, 10th Indian Infantry Division, quoted in Heinl, p. 197.

16. Brigadier General J. D. Hittle, USMC, in *The National Guardsman*, quoted in Heinl, p. 197.

17. John A. Lejeune, *Marine Corps Manual*, quoted in Heinl, p. 172.

18. Captain Sir Basil Liddell Hart, *Strategy*, quoted in Tsouras, pp. 291–292.

19. Colonel Ardant du Picq, *Battle Studies*, quoted in MCRP 6-11B, p. 21-30.

20. Ecclesiastes 1:9, quoted in MCRP 6-11B, p. 21-63.

21. Brigadier General S. L. A. Marshall, *The Armed Forces Officer*, quoted in Tsouras, p. 81.

22. U.S. Department of Defense, Department of the Navy, ALMAR 454/96, *Unit Cohesion—Commandant's Intent*, by General C. C. Krulak, Commandant of the Marine Corps, U.S. Marine Corps (Washington, D.C.: 1996).

23. Ibid.

24. Major General John A. Lejeune, *Marine Corps Manual*, quoted in MCRP 6-11B, p. 20-1.

25. ALMAR 454/96.

(reverse blank)

Made in the USA
Middletown, DE
02 June 2015